KUM🙂N
MATH. READING. SUCCESS.

What is Kumon?

Kumon is the world's largest supplemental education provider and a leader in producing outstanding results. After-school programs in math and reading at Kumon Centers around the globe have been helping children succeed for 50 years.

Kumon Workbooks represent just a fraction of our complete curriculum of preschool-to-college-level material assigned at Kumon Centers under the supervision of trained Kumon Instructors.

The Kumon Method enables each child to progress successfully by practicing material until concepts are mastered and advancing in small, manageable increments. Instructors carefully assign materials and pace advancement according to the strengths and needs of each individual student.

Students usually attend a Kumon Center twice a week and practice at home the other five days. Assignments take about twenty minutes.

Kumon helps students of all ages and abilities master the basics, improve concentration and study habits, and build confidence.

How did Kumon begin?

IT ALL BEGAN IN JAPAN 50 YEARS AGO when a parent and teacher named Toru Kumon found a way to help his son Takeshi do better in school. At the prompting of his wife, he created a series of short assignments that his son could complete successfully in less than 20 minutes a day and that would ultimately make high school math easy. Because each was just a bit more challenging than the last, Takeshi was able to master the skills and gain the confidence to keep advancing.

This unique self-learning method was so successful that Toru's son was able to do calculus by the time he was in the sixth grade. Understanding the value of good reading comprehension, Mr. Kumon then developed a reading program employing the same method. His programs are the basis and inspiration of those offered at Kumon Centers today under the expert guidance of professional Kumon Instructors.

Mr. Toru Kumon
Founder of Kumon

What can Kumon do for my child?

Kumon is geared to children of all ages and skill levels. Whether you want to give your child a leg up in his or her schooling, build a strong foundation for future studies or address a possible learning problem, Kumon provides an effective program for developing key learning skills given the strengths and needs of each individual child.

What makes Kumon so different?

Kumon uses neither a classroom model nor a tutoring approach. It's designed to facilitate self-acquisition of the skills and study habits needed to improve academic performance. This empowers children to succeed on their own, giving them a sense of accomplishment that fosters further achievement. Whether for remedial work or enrichment, a child advances according to individual ability and initiative to reach his or her full potential. Kumon is not only effective, but also surprisingly affordable.

What is the role of the Kumon Instructor?

Kumon Instructors regard themselves more as mentors or coaches than teachers in the traditional sense. Their principal role is to provide the direction, support and encouragement that will guide the student to performing at 100% of his or her potential. Along with their rigorous training in the Kumon Method, all Kumon Instructors share a passion for education and an earnest desire to help children succeed.

KUMON FOSTERS:

- A mastery of the basics of reading and math
- Improved concentration and study habits
- Increased self-discipline and self-confidence
- A proficiency in material at every level
- Performance to each student's full potential
- A sense of accomplishment

▶▶ GETTING STARTED IS EASY. Just call us at 877.586.6671 or visit kumon.com to request our free brochure and find a Kumon Center near you. We'll direct you to an Instructor who will be happy to speak with you about how Kumon can address your child's particular needs and arrange a free placement test. There are more than 1,700 Kumon Centers in the U.S. and Canada, and students may enroll at any time throughout the year, even summer. Contact us today.

FIND OUT MORE ABOUT KUMON MATH & READING CENTERS.
Receive a free copy of our parent guide, *Every Child an Achiever,* by visiting
kumon.com/go.survey or calling **877.586.6671**

Strawberry

To parents
Your child will gradually learn how to place each puzzle piece by judging its picture, color, shape, and number. Before your child starts pasting, encourage him or her to look carefully at the sample illustration on the right.

■ Cut out the parts along the ▬▬▬ lines and paste them onto the guide on the next page.

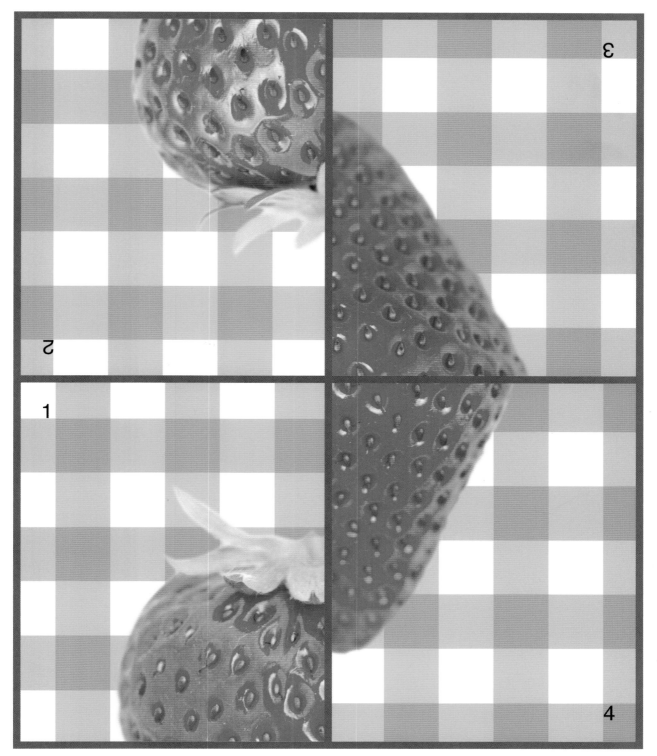

■ Arrange the parts from the previous page to complete the picture below.

Making Lunch

- Cut out the parts along the ▬▬▬▬ lines and paste them onto the guide on the next page.

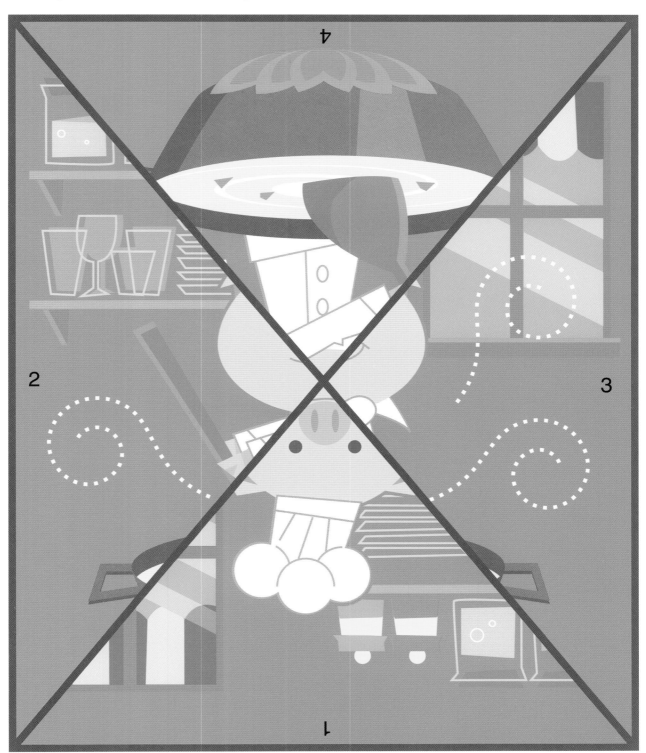

2 Making Lunch

■ Arrange the parts from the previous page to complete the picture below.

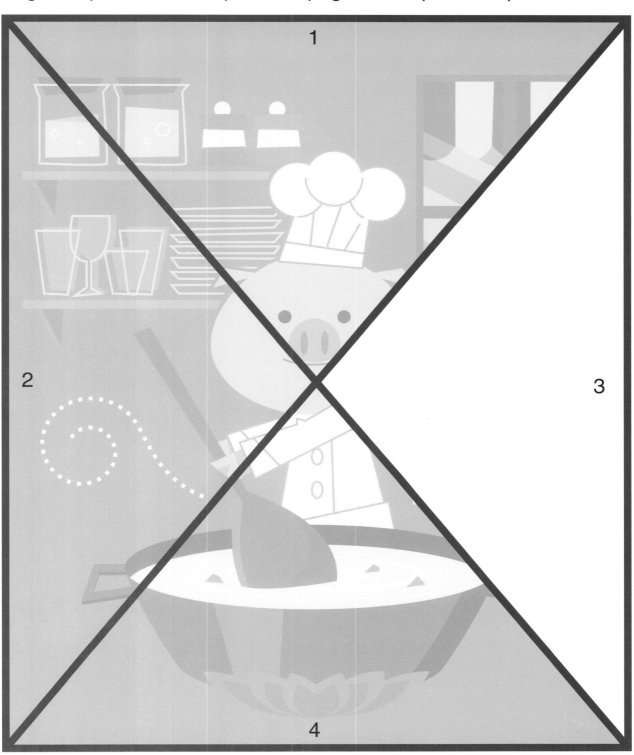

3 Space Shuttle

■ Cut out the parts along the ▬▬▬ lines and paste them onto the guide on the next page.

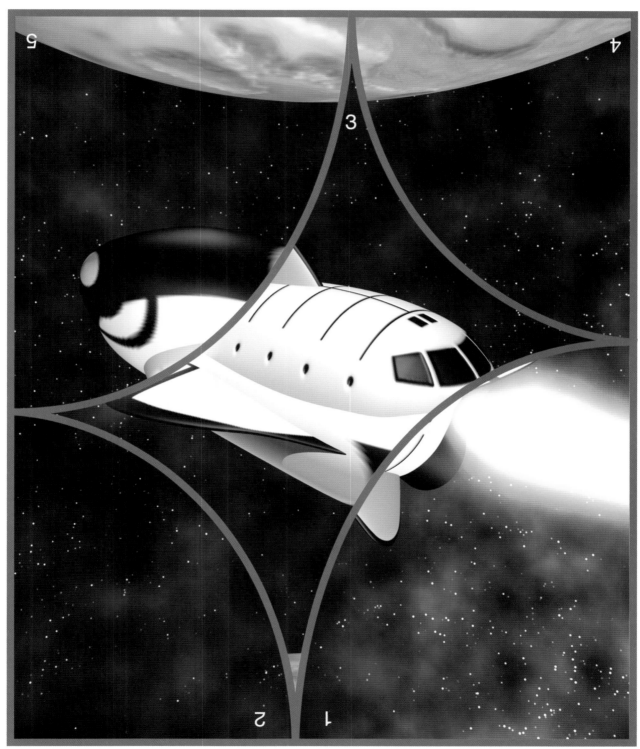

✳Parents, please cut along this line for your child.

Space Shuttle

■ Arrange the parts from the previous page to complete the picture below.

Elephant

■ Cut out the parts along the ▬▬▬ lines and paste them onto the guide on the next page.

4 Elephant

■ Arrange the parts from the previous page to complete the picture below.

To parents
In this exercise, each piece is the same shape. This will help emphasize the importance of considering the illustration when placing each part. Have your child look at the illustrated sections of the guide on the next page before he or she pastes the parts.

■ Cut out the parts along the ▬▬▬ lines and paste them onto the guide on the next page.

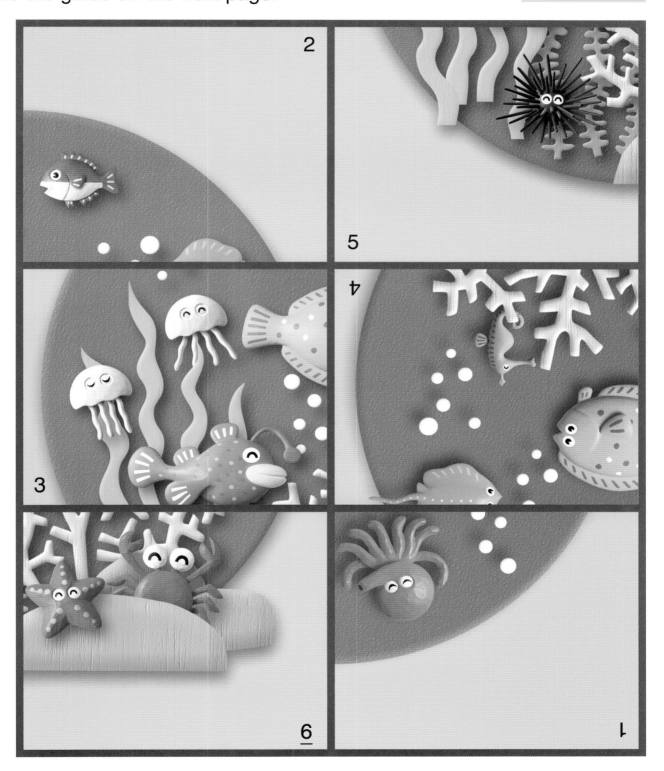

In the Sea

6 pieces

■ Arrange the parts from the previous page to complete the picture below.

1	2
3	4
5	6

 **Sports Time**

To parents
The cutting lines are becoming more difficult, and the number of pieces is slowly increasing. If your child seems to be having difficulty pasting the parts, you can offer to help. Offer lots of praise when he or she has completed the exercise.

■ Cut out the parts along the ▬▬▬ lines and paste them onto the guide on the next page.

Sports Time

■ Arrange the parts from the previous page to complete the picture below.

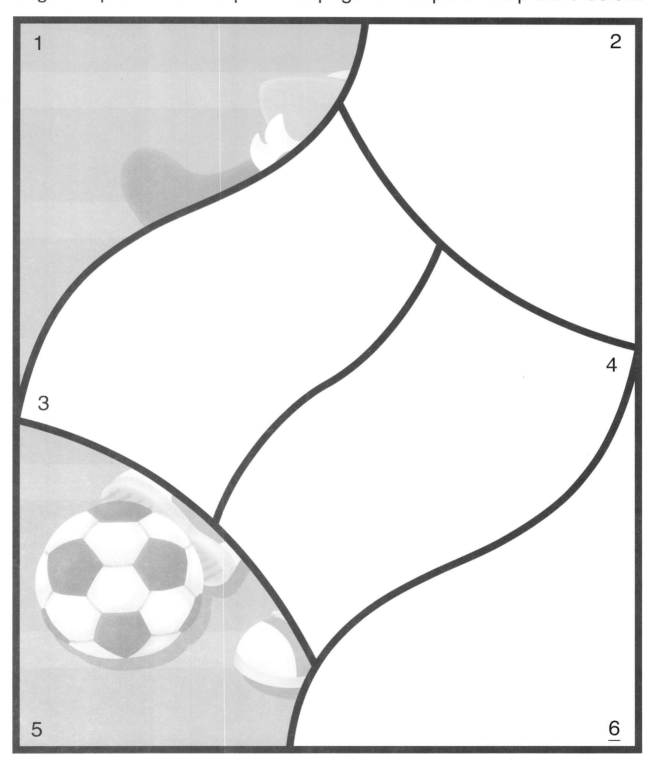

■ Cut out the parts along the ▬▬▬ lines and paste them onto the guide on the next page.

7 Fruit Tart

■ Arrange the parts from the previous page to complete the picture below.

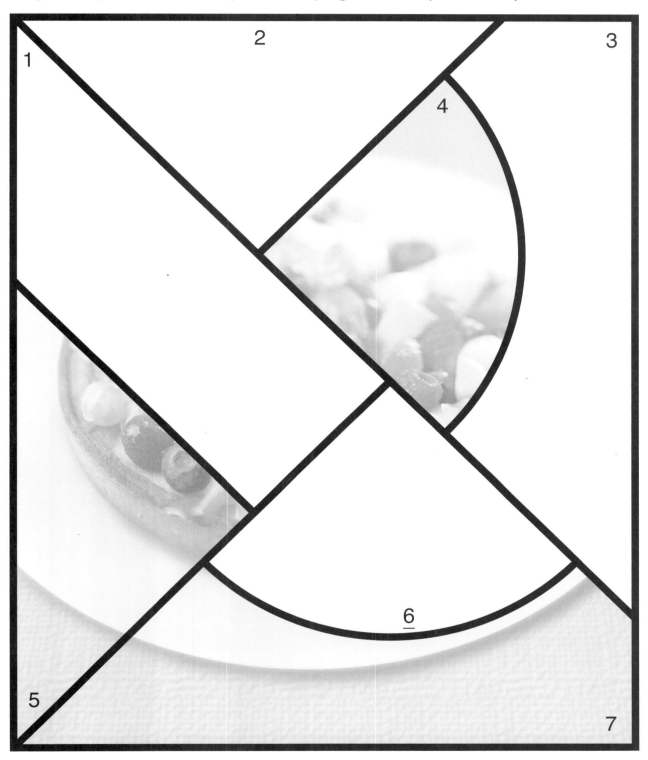

8 Happy Balloon

■ Cut out the parts along the ▬▬▬ lines and paste them onto the guide on the next page.

Happy Balloon

■ Arrange the parts from the previous page to complete the picture below.

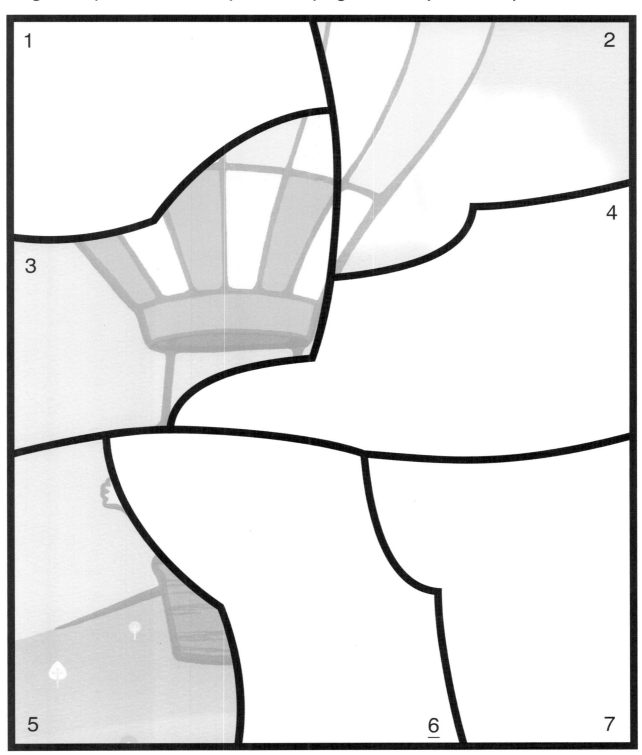

9 Dachshund

■ Cut out the parts along the ▬▬▬ lines and paste them onto the guide on the next page.

9 Dachshund

■ Arrange the parts from the previous page to complete the picture below.

Fantastical Forest

To parents
If your child is having difficulty with an exercise, you can offer to paste a couple of pieces in order to give him or her a hint. Please enjoy cutting and pasting together.

■ Cut out the parts along the ▬▬▬ lines and paste them onto the guide on the next page.

Fantastical Forest

■ Arrange the parts from the previous page to complete the picture below.

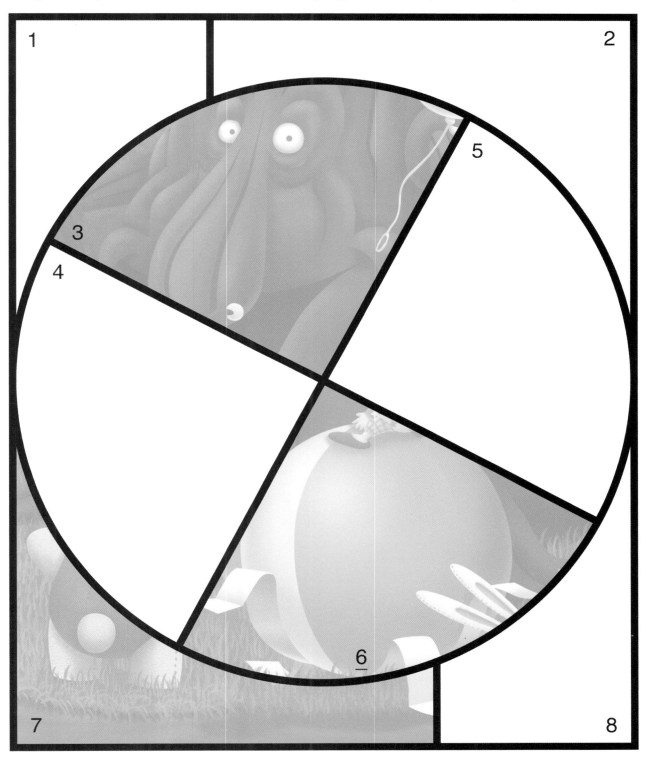

Nighttime Story

■ Cut out the parts along the ▬▬▬ lines and paste them onto the guide on the next page.

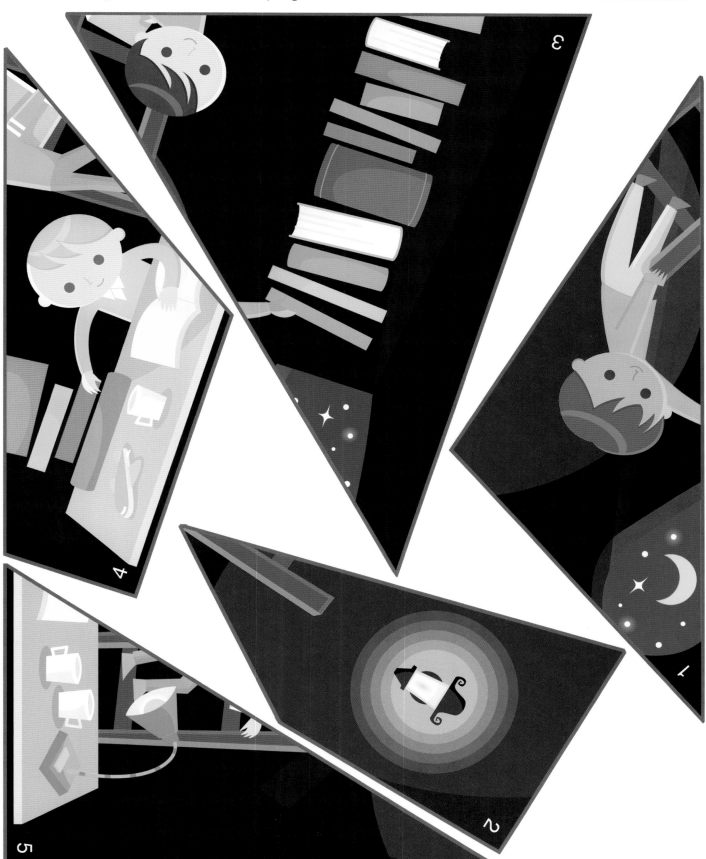

Nighttime Story

■ Arrange the parts from the previous page to complete the picture below.

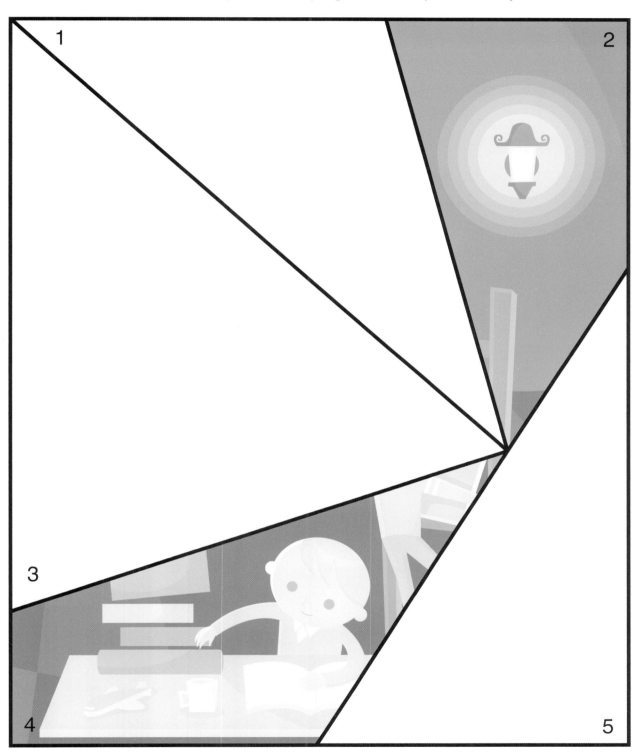

Jelly Beans

■ Cut out the parts along the ▬▬▬ lines and paste them onto the guide on the next page.

12

Jelly Beans

■ Arrange the parts from the previous page to complete the picture below.

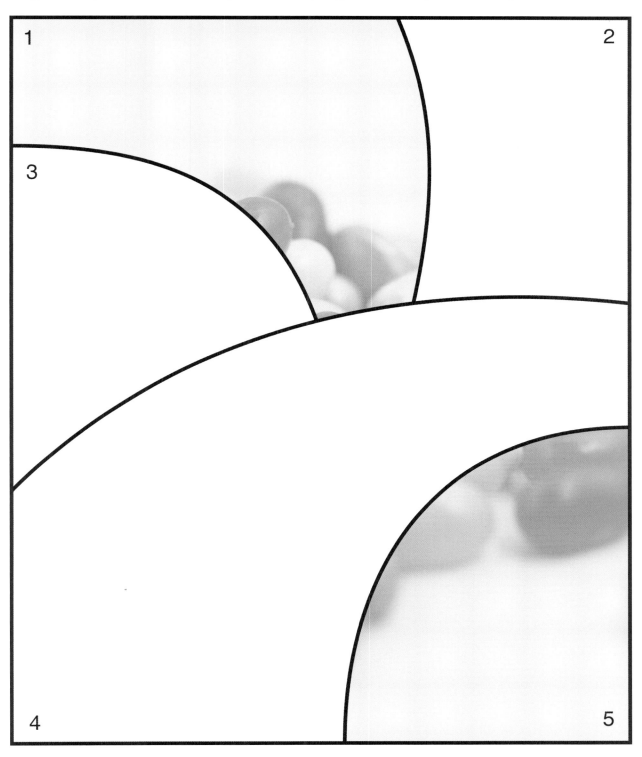

13 **Cruise Ship**

- Cut out the parts along the ▬▬▬ lines and paste them onto the guide on the next page.

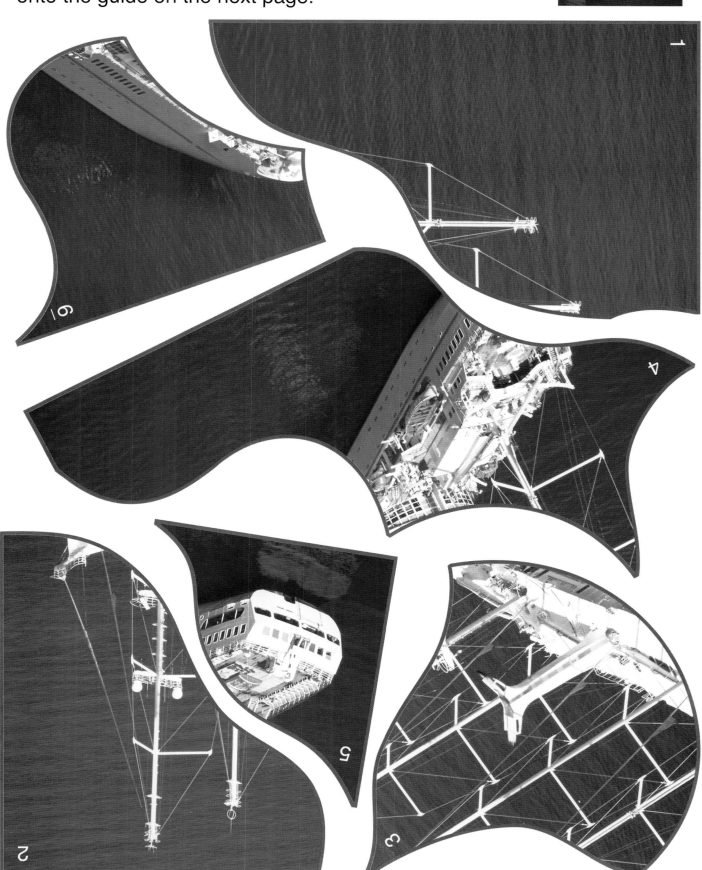

Cruise Ship

■ Arrange the parts from the previous page to complete the picture below.

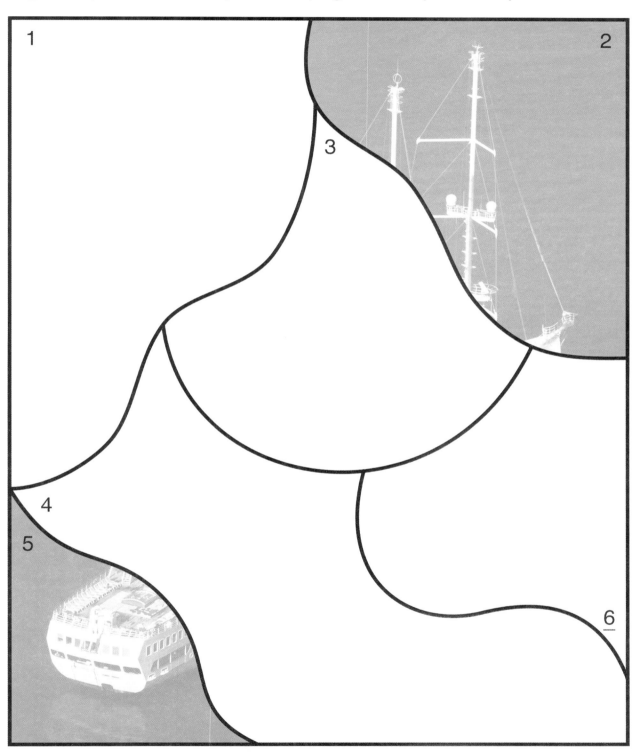

Picnic Fun

To parents
The shapes are now becoming a little more challenging. If your child seems to be having difficulty cutting them out, offer your help.

■ Cut out the parts along the ▬▬▬ lines and paste them onto the guide on the next page.

*Parents, please cut along this line for your child.

14

Picnic Fun

■ Arrange the parts from the previous page to complete the picture below.

The Magical Comet

■ Cut out the parts along the ▬▬ lines and paste them onto the guide on the next page.

The Magical Comet

■ Arrange the parts from the previous page to complete the picture below.

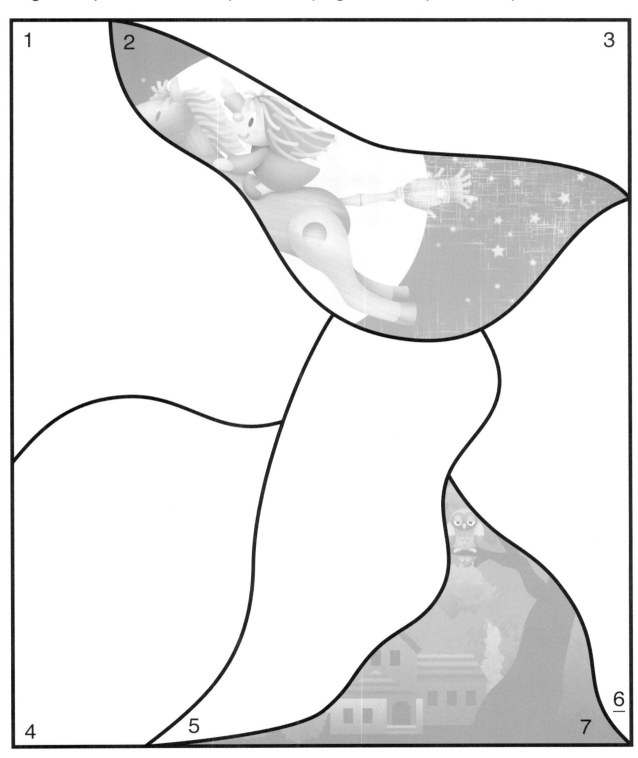

Zoo Train

Cut out the parts along the ▬▬▬ lines and paste them onto the guide on the next page.

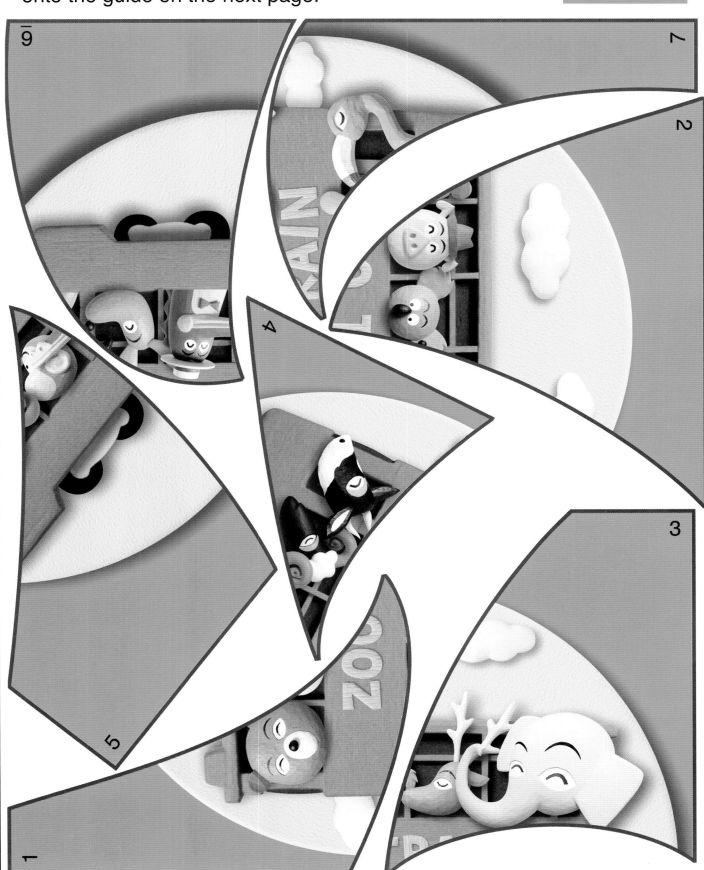

Zoo Train

■ Arrange the parts from the previous page to complete the picture below.

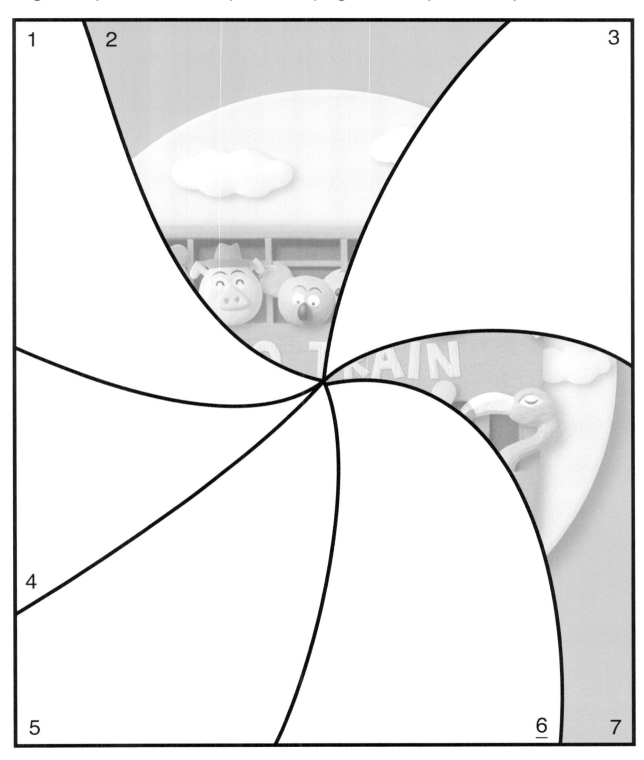

17 Tropical Beach

■ Cut out the parts along the ▬▬▬ lines and paste them onto the guide on the next page.

17 Tropical Beach

■ Arrange the parts from the previous page to complete the picture below.

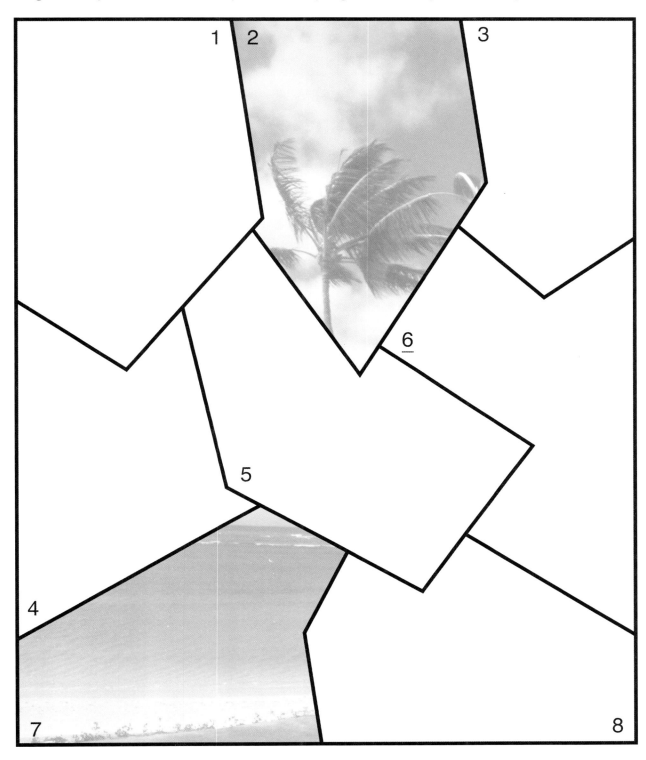

18 The Little Explorers

■ Cut out the parts along the ▬▬▬ lines and paste them onto the guide on the next page.

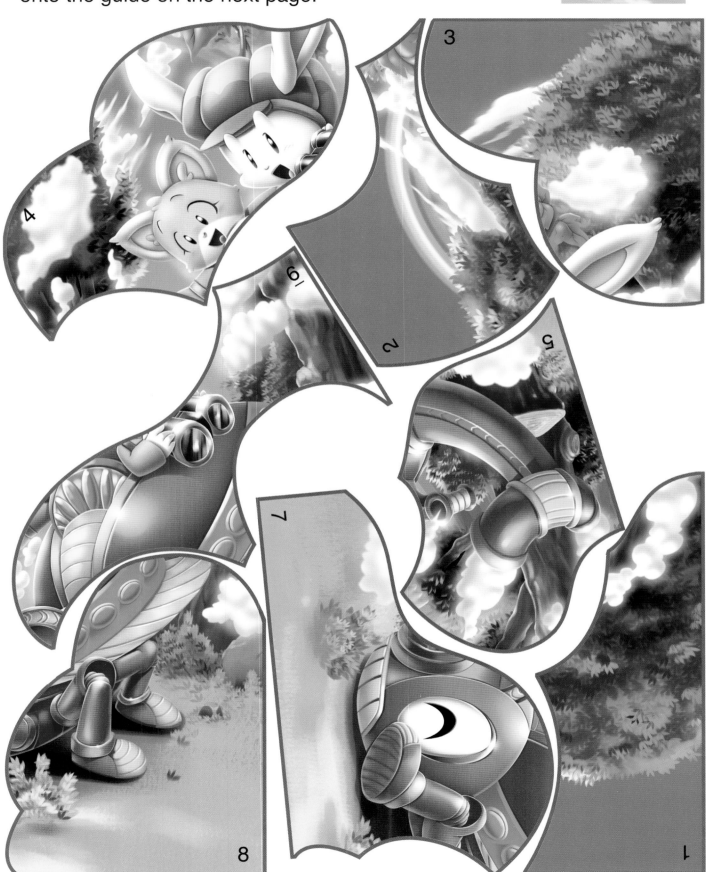

18 The Little Explorers

■ Arrange the parts from the previous page to complete the picture below.

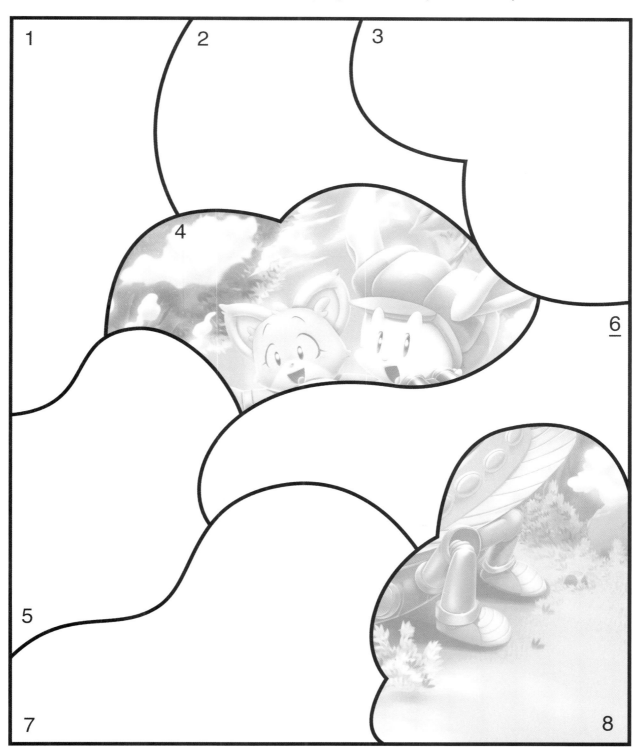

19 Lions

Cut out the parts along the ▬▬ lines and paste them onto the guide on the next page.

Lions

■ Arrange the parts from the previous page to complete the picture below.

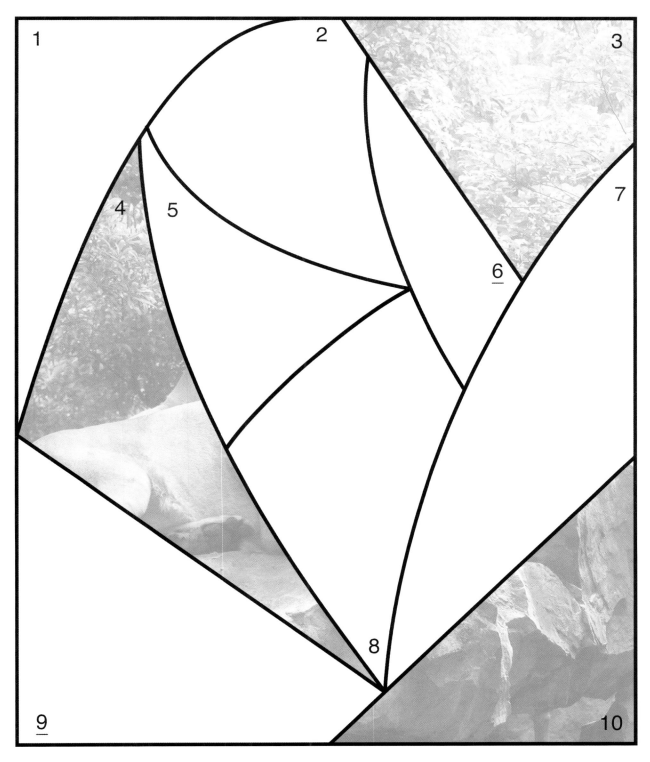

Finding a Lost Ladybug

20

To parents
This page is the most challenging page – placing the pieces may not be easy for your child. Offer your help if your child encounters difficulty. Hopefully you have enjoyed cutting and pasting these jigsaw puzzles with your child! Give your child lots of praise for his or her effort and achievement.

■ Cut out the parts along the ▬▬▬ lines and paste them onto the guide on the next page.

Finding a Lost Ladybug

■ Arrange the parts from the previous page to complete the picture below.

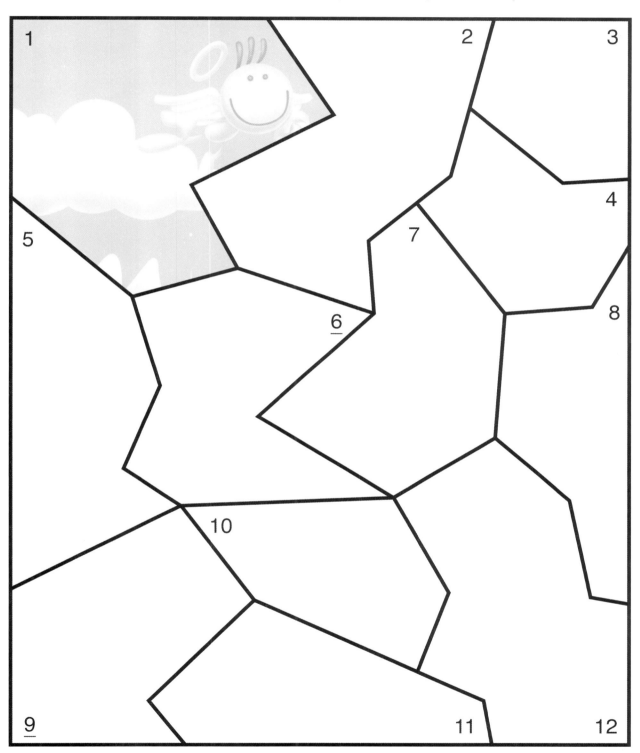

KUM☺N

Certificate of Achievement

is hereby congratulated on completing

My Book of Pasting: Jigsaw Puzzles

Presented on _____ , 20 _____

_____
Parent or Guardian